Musings Over A Mop Bucket:

Owning the music in local church worship

Philip McKenning

GILEAD
B O O K S
PUBLISHING

Gilead Books Publishing
Corner Farm
West Knapton
Malton
North Yorkshire YO17 8JB UK
www.GileadBooksPublishing.com

First published in Great Britain, May 2014
2 4 6 8 10 9 7 5 3 1

Copyright ©Philip McKenning 2014

British Library Cataloguing-in-Publication Data:
A catalogue record for this book is available from the British
Library.

ISBN: 978-0-9926713-3-4

All Scripture quotations are taken from the Holy Bible, New Living
Translation, copyright © 1996, 2004, 2007, 2013 by Tyndale
House Foundation. Used by permission of Tyndale House
Publishers, Inc., Carol Stream, Illinois 60188. All rights reserved.

The publisher makes every effort to ensure that the papers used
in our books are made from trees that have been legally sourced
from well-managed and credibly certified forests by using a
printer awarded FSC & PEFC chain of custody certification.

Cover design: Nathan Ward
Cover Illustration: ©Gill Douglas
Editor: David Burton

Contents

Introduction

Hello there.

I'm Phil. I'm 27 years old, a York resident, guitar teacher, worship leader and cleaner - bet you didn't see that coming - and now I'm an author too.

The catalyst for this book is simply that I am keen to see the expression of people's musical voice in church worship music.

When I started, I began by focusing on the subject of 'Finding Your Voice'. The aim was to explain what can be achieved if we let our creative voices come through to serve our churches' vision of worship.

However, after writing a few chapters it became clear to me that more thoughts were coming out than I was able to explore without going off the original theme. I decided to write a book of articles instead, which would allow me to cover all the ideas and practical solutions that had come out when I started writing.

I wanted to write a book that wouldn't take long to read, and that was broken into easily digestible chunks. This book includes theories, experiences, practical applications and workshop ideas which may be of assistance or just affirm thoughts you already have on this topic.

Please, understand that I am not wishing to instigate mutinies in your church worship teams. I don't want you to storm your worship leader's castle to bring down the regime of their worship dictatorship. We must support our leaders, and I am hoping that this book will be a help to our churches rather than a hindrance.

You don't have to agree with my viewpoints. It could be that in disagreeing with them, you find the answer to issues you are experiencing in your churches. If by you disagreeing with me, your church benefits, I'll be over the moon!

Finally, this is not a daily bible devotional; the scriptures at the top of each page add a biblical link to the theme of that current article. They are not there to support my opinions. My hope is that they may prod you to look in your Bible and read the book or chapter being quoted - never a bad thing!

All the best!
Philip McKenning

Chapter 1
Worship Ownership

So God created people in his own image; God patterned
them after himself; male and female he created them.
(Genesis 1:27)

There are times when I think 'aw, not this song! I hate playing this song!' Have you ever felt like that? It occurred to me the other day, though, that it's been a long time since I've been frustrated in a worship band context.

You can't like every worship song ever written. But I believe you can enjoy playing them. I've played in ABBA tribute concerts, and even though I wouldn't normally listen to ABBA by choice, I have really enjoyed playing those shows.

Before, I wouldn't have relished playing a worship song that I didn't like. Now, it's different because I have some creative input into the worship songs I play. I'm given the freedom to put my own stamp on those songs, just as other members of the band are. Consequently, when we play, it is a joint collaboration of musical and arrangement ideas, and it gives me and the band a sense that each song is ours.

The key word is 'ownership'. Musicians need creative influence in the worship music we play. As Christians we believe that God created the heavens and the earth and everything in it, which includes you and the music you make. I believe God is eager for us to embrace our individuality.

We know that God is creative, and that we are made in his image – and therefore we know that we are creative and our music also must be. Go to any art gallery or cathedral, minster or abbey and see the breadth of art and architecture that has been inspired to show the world God's glory! Look through any old hymnals and read the depth of poetry dedicated to sharing his good news, or listen to the many composers of classical music, whose music is stirred by God – Handel's Messiah is an obvious starting place.

O nations of the world, recognize the Lord; recognize that the Lord is glorious and strong. Give to the Lord the glory he deserves! Bring your offering and come to worship him. (Psalm 96:7-9)

We point to Jesus and his majesty in worship; should we not embrace our musical originality – which he designed us with – in service to him?

As I conclude this first chapter, here is a question that's just presented itself to me:

How much modern art and mainstream popular music is devoted to the magnificence of God?

Chapter 2
Finding your Voice

Sing a new song to the Lord!
Let the whole earth sing to the Lord!
(Psalm 96:1)

Firstly, what is our voice? Our musical voice is what is known as our style or sound.

I'm sure many of us can identify a particular band or artist just by listening to a recording, even though we may never have heard that particular song before. The reason for this is that they have a distinctive sound; and we should be no different.

Your voice is you. It's your sound. It's that unique thing which means that when someone hears you express yourself musically on a recording, in church, in a band, even busking on the street, they can say, 'That's Jim!' You can tell. I can hear it. 'There's that blend of Eric Clapton and Jimmy Page with a touch of Carlos Santana. I'd know his guitar sound anywhere!'

Our voice is a culmination of all those musicians

whose influence we've chosen to apply to our playing. The type of music we love, the music teachers we've had, the music we've listened to, and the songs we've covered, all make up our musical genetics.

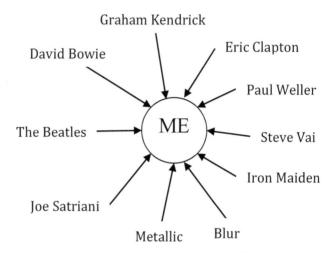

Fig. 1 Musical Influences

As can be seen in fig. 1, I have put down some influences that I have put into my guitar playing, and in some cases, my singing. Certain parts of my playing may involve scales, chord shapes and sounds that are used by these bands. They can also be heard in my song-writing methods or my vocal style in certain songs.

Something I must make clear is that music is

subjective. Everyone is different, and so just as no two singing voices are the same, no two *musical* voices are the same either. This is awesome, because it means that we all have something special and unique to bring to our music teams. I believe that as musicians serving our churches, we should be true to our tastes.

Hang on! Don't panic. I'm not saying we should play whatever we like in church and the congregation can just make do. We are there to help the congregation in their worship to God. That is our job. We should be true to our voice, whilst being appropriate to the contexts we are playing in. You wouldn't have a doom metal band performing in a jazz club. (Although saying that, I'm sure you could make a jazz/doom metal hybrid and I for one would be interested in hearing it!)

LISTEN! In order to get some influences in the first place we must listen to music. As an electric guitarist I naturally gravitate to music that has electric guitar as its focus. When you're developing your 'voice', listening to music which involves your instrument is a great place to start.

Like I said, your voice is you. In order to unlock your musical voice you need to nourish yourself with music that you find inspiring and enjoyable.

Remember that Jack Black film, 'School Of Rock'? At one point in the film it's the end of a school day, and Jack Black, the teacher, has a pile of CDs which he passes out to his class, telling them that they're going to listen to some real music. Then he gives classic rock albums to each student who would benefit from them. So the keyboard player is given a Yes album, and told to listen to Rick Wakeman's keyboard solo on the song 'Roundabout'. The drummer gets the Rush album '2112' so he can listen to Neil Peart's drumming. The singer is given the 'Parallel Lines' album by Blondie to listen to. The guitarist gets 'Axis: Bold As Love' by the Jimi Hendrix Experience - I myself would've gone with 'Electric Ladyland' but hey! That's my preference; my voice. I don't recall the bass player getting a CD, but I imagine it could have been a Cream album featuring the legendary bass-playing of Jack Bruce. Again, just my preference.

In the film, the students study rock 'family trees', showing which bands are connected and how they link up the various genres of rock. In doing this the students can see the roots of the bands they love, and can indulge in further listening and acquire more influences. They also watch video clips of great rock musicians to see how they perform and present themselves on stage.

Agreed, in a worship context, smashing up your equipment, setting fire to your guitar or playing the organ with your feet like Keith Emerson is not the target. We are supposed to be pointing to Jesus and his story – not to the fact that we can play the guitar with our teeth whilst doing the splits! However, there is a lot we can learn by examining other musicians' approaches.

My vicar told me that in order to grow and improve as a leader it would be good for me to watch videos of worship leaders leading, and read books they had written. I have to say it was good advice and time well spent, though I still have much to learn. Worship leaders have to develop their own leading style and voice too, in order to be authentic to the people they are leading.

We are fortunate that at the click of a button we have access to oceans of useful information – such as internet streaming, mp3s and social media – to help us evolve our voices.

Something I like to do for myself, and encourage others to do in my capacity as a guitar teacher and worship musician, is to select a favourite musician and do a case study on their playing. I listed five favourite guitarists and then looked into the specific scales or techniques they used, styles they played with and FXs or amp settings they incorporated into their music – basically, anything they did that really excited me as a player. Then I would work to add those ingredients into my own playing, expanding my voice.

Now, just because I understand and have learned how Eric Clapton plays doesn't mean I am Eric Clapton. I can recreate his sound and feel, but I don't have his musical brain or his hands. It's still me – and that includes a bit of Eric Clapton's style. Since I have a love for many other guitarists, their playing is integrated into my voice too.

These influences mix with the Clapton in my playing, as Clapton mixes with them; and these fuse into something else, which becomes my own unique voice. If we were to look at Clapton's influences we would find that his style is a fusion of guitarists like BB King, Muddy Waters, Freddie King, Albert King, Robert Johnson and many more. EC would have also learned things from his contemporaries – Jimi Hendrix, Jeff Beck and Jimmy Page, to name just a few.

There's a thought. In our churches we are part of a team of musicians with varied musical tastes, experience and knowledge. We would be silly not to tap into that and learn as much as we can from one another.

Chapter 3
Bring and Share Music

And all the believers met together constantly
and shared everything they had.
(Acts 2:44)

As a church musician, I am always surprised to find that some of my fellow players seem to lack a proper interest in the art they are creating! Many times I have heard musicians say, 'I play, but I don't listen to music.'

My response goes something like this: 'I'm sorry you don't listen...what? You really...? But...*why*?'

As you can tell, I'm baffled by this, and I once decided that it would be profitable to have a worship team evening where we would bring and share music with each other. It was called, simply, 'Bring and Share Music'. The plan for the evening was that members of the team would bring a recording of a song or piece of music that they love or were just really into at that moment, and share it with each other. I should say that the music wasn't just 'Christian' – although I did stipulate nothing inappropriate.

The team was split into listening groups, which consisted of a variety of ages and congregational teams. We have a large team that spans across four congregations, and each team has its own specific style of worship to accommodate the congregation they are serving. As you can imagine, we had a diverse variety of music to listen to. We listened to genres ranging from classical to heavy metal. From Handel to Killswitch Engage.

The groups would listen to about a minute and a half of each other's music and then discuss it. I furnished each group with question sheets to help their discussions. You can see the sheet layout on the next page if you fancy giving it a go yourselves.

The worship team had an enjoyable time and good discussions, and we were able to acknowledge each other's musical differences. I feel it really helped to bring a closer unity to the four congregational teams. In the long run I'm hoping that things like this will help us to accept each other's musical preferences more. Then, in time, we will explore how they might be incorporated into a worship setting.

Fig. 2 – Bring And Share Discussion Sheet

TRACK TITLE:

ARTIST NAME:

1. ANY THOUGHTS:

2. DOES OUR WORSHIP INCORPORATE ANY
ASPECTS OF THIS?

3. COULD ASPECTS OF THIS BE INCORPORATED
INTO OUR WORSHIP?

Chapter 4
Recommended Listening

Then Jesus called to the crowd to come and hear.
All of you listen, he said, and try to understand.
(Mark 7:14)

'Christian' music is not Christian for the music but for the message. So whatever Christian music you listen to, it will be a strand of a particular genre. If you've decided that the best way to edify yourself is only to listen to Christian music, then believe it or not pretty much every genre is covered.

And so, I decided to ask my church's worship team and my friends and family what their favourite Christian albums are, add few tips of my own, and list them for you to look into. Enjoy!

Fig. 3 Recommended Listening Album List

CCM

10,000 Reasons - Matt Redman
CompassionArt - Various
Simply Worship 3 - Hillsongs Australia
Opposite Way - Leeland
Open - YFriday
When Silence Falls - Tim Hughes
Much Afraid - Jars Of Clay
Cannons - Phil Wickham
The Hurt And The Healer - MercyMe
A New Hallelujah - Michael W. Smith
Through The Valley - Lex Buckley
For The Sake Of The Call - Stephen Curtis Chapman
Oxygen - Avalon
Restored - Jeremy Camp
See What A Morning - Chris Tomlin
All Of The Above - Hillsong United
The Power Of One - Israel Houghton
Fearless - Philips, Craig & Dean
Come Away - Jesus Culture
Leaving Eden - Brandon Heath
The Reckoning - NeedToBreathe
Where I Find You - Kari Jobe
Blessings - Laura Story
A Messenger - Colton Dixon

Nothing Is Wasted - Elevation Worship

Pop

Black And White - Royal Tailor
Morning Like This - Sandi Patti
Revival In This Land - Carman
Beyond A Dream - Twila Paris
Take Me To Your Leader - Newsboys
Butterfly Kisses (Shades Of Grace) - Bob Carlisle
Jaci Velasquez - Jaci Velasquez
Six Pence None The Richer - Six Pence None The Richer
The Promise - Plus One
Stacie Orrico - Stacei Orrico
Dance Or Die - Family Force 5
The Lost Get Found - Britt Nicole
The Light Meets The Dark - Tenth Avenue North
My Paper Heart - Francesca Battistelli
Eye On It - Toby Mac

Country

Nuff Said - Tommy Brandt
Amazing Grace - BJ Thomas
The Way Home - Russ Taff
Life, Love And Other Mysteries - Point Of Grace
The Gift - Kenny Rogers
You Light Up My Life - LeAnn

Rimes

Let Freedom Ring - Bill & Gloria Gaither

Rise And Shine - Randy Travis

Precious Memories - Alan Jackson

Songs Of Inspiration - Alabama

Get Away, Jordan - Ernie Hasse & Signature Sound

Downtown Church - Patty Griffin

Real Life - Lincoln Brewster

Rock

Love Without Measure - Parachute Band

Ending Is Beginning - Downhere

Kings Kaleidoscope - Sin

Jesus Freak - DC Talk

King Of Fools - Delirious?

Beautiful Letdown - Switchfoot

Give Us Rest - Dave Crowder Band

Mmhmm - Relient K

Not Of This World - Petra

Human Clay - Creed

Time - Third Day

Underdog - Audio Adrenaline

To Know That You're Alive – Kutless

Gospel

Salvation Station - New World Son

Some People Change - Michael English

The Sound - MaryMary

One More Song For You - The Imperials

In His Time Praise IV - The Marantha Singers

Kirk Franklin & Family - Kirk Franklin & Family

God Is Working - Brooklyn Tabernacle Choir

Mountain High...Valley Low - Yolanda Adams

Love And Freedom - BeBe Winans

Live In London And More - Donnie McClurkin

Throne Room - CeCe Winans

Something Bout Love - Fred Hammond

Bless The Broken Road - Selah

True Beauty - Mandisa

Tell Me What You Know - Sarah Groves

Audience Of One - Heather Headley

Ska

Our Newest Album Ever - Five Iron Frenzy

Blues

Love From A Distance - Joe Lewis Band

The Water And The Blood – Sojourn

Celtic

Beyond These Shores - Iona

Mortal – Fathom

Folk
Campfire - Rend Collective Experiment
Caedmon's Call - Caedmon's Call
Lay It Down - Jennifer Knapp

Jazz
Mark Edwards Swing Gospel Jazz Orchestra

Progressive
3 Cheers For The Broken Hearted - Glass Hammer

Hip-Hop
13 Letters - 116 Clique
Between Two Worlds - Trip Lee
Rehab - Lecrae
Blacklight - Tedashii
Weight And Glory - KP
Heroes For Sale - Andy Mineo

Singer/Songwriter
Every Place Is Under The Stars - Adrian Snell
Light In The Darkest Nights - Steph Macleod
I Have A Hope - Tommy Walker
Paid On The Nail - Graham Kendrick
Beautiful Things - Gungor
Seven Swans - Sufjan Stevens
I Saw The Lord - Dallas Holm

Anything Worth Saying - Aaron Shust
City Of Black N White - Mat Kearney

Metal
Eye Of The Storm - Divinefire
Psych Surgery - Tourniquet
Anhedonia - Teramaze
Brainchild - Circle Of Dust
Satellite - P.O.D.
Fallen - Evanescence
O God, The Aftermath - Norma Jean
Southern Weather - The Almost
Messengers - August Burns Red
Roots Above & Branches Below - Devil Wears Prada
Horseshoes & Handgrenades - Disciple
The End Is Where We Begin - 1000 Year Krutch
Immortal - For Today
Human Sacrifice - Vengeance Rising
Where Blood & Fire Bring Rest - Zao
Detonation - Blood Good
Deliverance - Deliverance
Pillars Of Humanity - The Crucified

Chapter 5
Inclusion not Exclusion

*The Lord said to Gideon, "You have too many warriors
with you. With these three hundred men I will rescue
you and give you victory over the Midianites."*
(Judges 7:2a, 7:7a)

The message in this opening scripture reminds us that
God can do much with a little. Many of our churches
will not have an abundance of resources, but as we
see in the Bible, God helps the weak and makes much
out of the small. The story of Gideon is one of my
favourite examples. Did you know that the Israelites
began with an army of thirty-two thousand? Now just
three hundred were pitted against, and I quote from
Judges 7:12:

> *The armies of Midian, Amalek, and the people of
> the east had settled in the valley like a swarm of
> locusts. Their camels were like grains of sand on
> the seashore-too many to count!*

The result was that God gave the Israelites victory over Midian!

We may be blessed with only a few musicians, and perhaps they don't even form a standard band, but know this: we are blessed!

Imagine this scenario. You're in a church music group containing a traditional church organ, a couple of singers and a flute. Then there's a young teenager who has taken up the drums.

To some that would be a ludicrous mix of musicians for a worship team. To me that has very exciting possibilities! And think, if this teenager's drumming can be included, how many secret musicians might turn out to be hiding in the congregation?

I'm an electric guitarist, and if I saw a worship team with a church organ, a flute and some singers, I might initially think there would be no place for my instrument in that set-up. Now, if I see a drummer up there, I think, 'wait – this team is willing to use anything to worship regardless of the narrow boxes that genres in music may stipulate'. If there's a drummer up there, you may find that a bassist appears and so on. The team grows.

Excited? Do you see the possibilities when we are inclusive rather than exclusive?

No doubt many of you are doing this, and have been doing it forever, and that's wonderful. But how can we start doing it?

Chapter 6
Worship Team Auditions

Now all of you together are Christ's body, and each one
of you is a separate and necessary part of it.
(1 Corinthians 12:27)

Just to clarify: when I say 'inclusive', I don't mean 'free-for-all'!

There are certain obstacles to these hybrid ensembles. We must work out how to play together effectively, so it doesn't become a horrible mess.

I believe there needs to be a little bit of a security check – nothing fancy, just an informal audition, for two reasons. First, to make sure that it is right for each person to serve. And second, to make sure that they are up to the musical standard that you require. Simple.

My worship director told me a story once about how he was caught out whilst at another church. Someone had joined the church and expressed an interest in joining the music group. They indicated that they had been heavily involved in leading worship at their previous church, and so my director welcomed them in, no questions asked. Who wouldn't?

After one service it became evident to my director that he'd made a mistake, and that they weren't really up to it. He had to go through the difficult process of saying this, and thus removing them from the team.

All this could have been avoided if there was an audition first. My director handled this extremely well and they have remained firm friends.

As a worship coordinator, my co-worship coordinator and I have only had to inform one person after an audition that they weren't musically up to the standard, and though it wasn't a pleasant experience, we received some wise advice from our worship director which helped us to make it constructive.

His advice was to:

A. Explain the reasons why we felt they didn't fit at the moment
B. Encourage them, and not leave them despairing
C. Offer them an opportunity to try again.

A. The reason was that their skills weren't good enough to cope with the demand of being in the worship bands on Sunday. It would have been too difficult, and probably a little humiliating, for them.

It also would have been difficult for the worship leader, who would have had expectations of higher ability, and would consequently have found himself in a difficult position.

B. We had put together a folder of popular worship songs that we frequently played on a Sunday. We gave it to them, to encourage them to develop their musical gifts, and to help them practice. We also suggested other musical opportunities that were available in the church for them to be part of, such as the gospel choir.

C. We explained that if they got to grips with the songs in the folder, and felt they had improved to a point where they would like to audition again, then they would be most welcome.

It is important to say that when you're meeting with a potential new recruit, you should make them aware that it is an audition. Informal, yes, but the person should be aware that they may not be asked to join the team.

Most of the time, the person will know after the audition whether they are out of their depth, and decide whether they are still interested.

An audition usually lasts from twenty to thirty minutes. We begin and end with prayer, asking God for guidance and direction. Then we explain the commitments involved in being part of the team, discuss the person's availability and other practicalities. We would then talk about their Christian and musical background, and finally play through a few songs that are used on a Sunday.

When selecting these songs, it is good to cover as many styles as possible. We tended to pick a hymn, a praise song and a reflective song. Sometimes, depending on the instrument, we would pick songs that lent themselves more to that particular instrument. For bass players, we liked to use 'When I Was Lost (There Is A New Song)' by Kate Simmonds, because it's funky and involves walking bass lines. This would be the most complex song a bassist would have to tackle, and likely the bass would be expected to drive the song in performance.

We decided that it was best never to inform a candidate of our decision then and there, because we needed to discuss our collective decision. It's also often beneficial to have time to reflect and seek God some more.

It is very important to tell the candidate when you will be telling them your decision. Normally, we would let them know in a week's time.

It's very rewarding to be able to audition and bring people onto the team, and it's exciting to see how your new recruit impacts your team dynamic and your church's worship. Never underestimate that potential.

Chapter 7
Non-Christian Musicians

And I heard a voice say, 'Get up, Peter; kill and eat
them.' 'Never, Lord,' I replied. 'I have never eaten
anything forbidden by our Jewish laws.'
But the voice from heaven came again, 'If God says
something is acceptable, don't say it isn't.'
(Acts 11:7-9)

It's only been recently that I have changed my opinion on whether non-Christian musicians should be part of the worship group. For a long time, I had the view that worship musicians must be Christians, end of story.

While I was a worship coordinator, my worship director challenged me on this point. I was asking him for guidance about worship group auditions, and the topic came up. I was taken aback to find that in his opinion it was okay for non-Christians to the join the team.

I debated with him over a number of conversations, and sought the opinions of my fellow worship-practitioners.

I couldn't understand his viewpoint. How can you be part of something dedicated to helping others glorify and engage with God if you are not doing it yourself?

My worship director said that although he would not allow a non-Christian to lead worship in a service, he would allow them to play in the band, provided they agreed with the worship team's ethic and were committed.

I was still of the opinion that it's impossible to be committed to something you don't believe in. He explained that a musician might like to be involved in a worship group for the community, and the social aspects of playing music, regardless of their religious beliefs. He went on to say that this might be their only experience of church, and that in a worship context they would be exposed to one of the most powerful ways in which the church points to Jesus – and he shouldn't be hindered in experiencing it.

I couldn't fault his logic. Everything is redeemable if God chooses to make it so. God worked through unbelievers for His glory and purposes in the Bible, for instance in the story of Rahab (See Joshua Chapter 2).

Chapter 8
Frequency Avoidance

Only Luke is with me. Get Mark and bring him with you,
because he is helpful to me in my ministry.
(2 Timothy 4:11)

I was once at a Christian conference, where I attended some worship seminars. One seminar was a 'Playing in a band' workshop. They had the basic worship band setup: keys, drums, bass, acoustic, electric, percussion and vocals. During the course of the session, those running the workshop played through various songs and explained what each musician was playing and how they related to each other, their use of worship hand signals, and so on.

Nothing wrong with that, nothing wrong at all; in fact it was led very well indeed. Where's the issue? Well, some of you who are reading this will know already, just as one bloke did in the seminar. I didn't cotton on to it until he pointed it out and it was a light-bulb moment for me.

This bloke raised his hand as a confused student would do after the teacher had explained arithmetic. The man's hand was spotted and the workshop leader opened the floor for his question. The man, let's call him Steve, responded thus:

'That's alright for you, but what do you do if your church band has an organ, drums, fiddle and acoustic guitar? What then?'

The leader responded, 'We're just showing you one way, Steve, it's not exclusive – some of these things are transferrable.'

Completely true; they are. However, there wasn't the time to explain what those things were, and how they might be transferrable – which was a shame, as I believe the majority of Churches in the UK will not have such a clear-cut set of musicians serving on their worship teams.

A couple of years ago I had the privilege of being in charge of the music and worship for a new congregation at my church. This involved building a team of musicians from the members of that congregation.

One of the main challenges with this team was working out the rota. How could I cover the musical requirements for the worship in the congregation whilst making sure that each member of the music team had regular breaks from playing and so was able to receive in the pews as well as giving out on stage?

One week I might have a 'normal' worship band – drums, bass, keys and acoustic guitar. In another, I may not have had a bass, or have been without drummer, or had just keys and a string section.

Some of you reading will be thinking 'I wish I had that many options,' and I agree I was spoilt, but it was still important to get the various combinations to work well.

Perhaps you have encountered similar scenarios. When there were gaps, the question for me was, 'what can these musicians play to make up for the missing frequencies or instruments? What styles can this band cover effectively?'

During my time as worship coordinator, I was able to do some music workshops covering these questions, so I'll endeavour to do the same here.

Here are some real-life scenarios, with explanations. Hopefully they will be of some help.

Scenario 1: Drums, Keys (Leader), Viola, Backing Vocals

Missing instrument - bass.

The keys can cover the missing bass frequencies. In order to achieve this, it would be useful for the keys player to play down an octave with their left hand. Since the keys are the lead instrument, the keys player's right hand should stay nearer middle C, and not stray into higher frequencies. In this set-up, there's no room for accompaniment or twiddling as far as the keys are concerned. The keyboard player's main jobs in this band are to cover the missing bass frequencies and fill out the mid-range.

The viola can add some embellishments, and on occasion mirror the melody and other written lines found on the lead sheets. It will also lend the worship a more folky edge.

The drums will be the driving force when it's needed for more upbeat songs, and will create a solid foundation. The drummer had the freedom to be a bit flamboyant in this band to help fill out the sound and add some presence.

The backing vocalists can add depth to choruses and support the lead vocal. With some careful arranging there could be opportunities for the viola and backing vocals to blend together.

I'd like to think that, with some thought to style and arrangement, no type of song is off-limits no matter what the band.

Scenario 2: Acoustic Guitar (Leader), Acoustic Guitar, Percussion/Trumpet

This really did happen and I was leading on acoustic guitar. We are missing many things.

What we did with the acoustic guitars was to play the same rhythms. More sound is better in an ensemble like this, and playing the same rhythms added strength and helped keep things tight. I also added bass notes to my playing to add a bit of bottom end. The other acoustic was played with a capo to add a clear distinction between the acoustic guitars.

Percussion was a cajon or box drum, and it mainly re-created the thump of a kick drum. I believe we had a tambourine and some shakers to add a bit more rhythm in louder sections and ambience in the more quieter moments.

The trumpet was used for embellishments, and only in quieter songs which were less rhythmically dependent.

We played 'We Believe' by Graham Kendrick, which worked well in that set-up. For this ensemble I picked more songs that would work with upbeat strumming; Be Thou My Vision was another choice.

Scenario 3: Electric Guitar (Leader), Bass, Drums

I was leading again, and I love leading from electric guitar! One of my favourite bands is Cream and I love playing in a 3-piece, so I set up the rota for this especially.

I played the electric guitar, using barre chords and solid rhythms. In upbeat songs, I used more heavy sounds like overdrive and distortion, and played more chord-based riffs. In the quieter songs I may have used some chorus FXs and delay, and played by plucking the chord changes or accenting them with strums, whilst leaving the bass and drums to drive the music. I was keen for the bass and drums to be very busy. I wanted a lot of sound, and for the music to have a strong, driving feel.

This was during a time when we were using songs like 'The Greatest Day in History' (Tim Hughes) and 'Water You Turned into Wine' (Chris Tomlin), and the band was set up for a rockier time of worship. We also played 'Light of The World' (Tim Hughes), which sounded more like a rock ballad.

Scenario 4: Drums, Bass, Keys, Acoustic (leader), Acoustic, Electric x2, Trumpet, Viola, Violin x2, Percussion, Backing Vocals x3

This band was my complete team. Some of the rota gaps were filled by people I had seconded from other teams. I wanted it to be celebration of all we had achieved so far.

We played mainly upbeat praise songs that service, which was the Mother's Day service. I had to spend a lot of time writing out arrangement sheets for the whole band, in order to separate the different instruments. I had a rule: 'if you're not sure what to play, don't play.'

It was a brilliant experience. I can't be sure if the band followed my arrangement sheets or not, because there was so much sound going on. But they seemed to follow the dynamics well, which was basically all my sheets depicted for the each section of each song.

That's the idea, and there are plenty of resources out there that can help you play effectively as a band. Paul Baloche does a great video which can be found on the internet covering this too.[1]

The main challenge is covering the missing frequencies, or avoiding each other's frequencies. If you're missing a bass, who can make up the low-end?

If you've got an electric guitar and a keyboard, who plays in the low-mid range and who plays in the high-mid range? Or do you thicken the sound by having guitar and keys play in the same frequency?

These are decisions that a leader may have to make when arranging a band, but why not help them out by making that decision yourselves, by listening to one another and to what the song needs. You don't have to play all the time; your part may have more impact if you wait till the pre-chorus before you come in.

Since it's likely that you don't have the luxury of doing hours of daily rehearsals, then being able to answer these questions instinctively will be no end of help to your rehearsal times, your worship leader and ultimately your church.

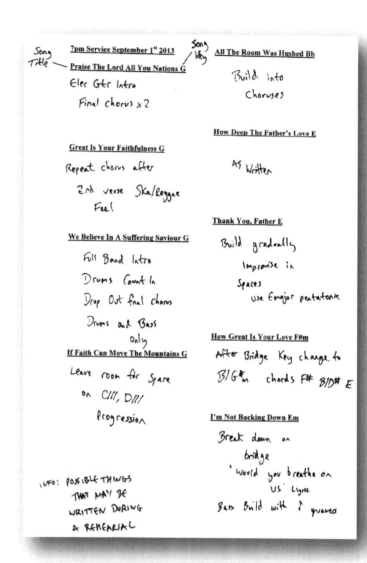

Song Title ——

7pm Service September 1st 2013

Song Key

Praise The Lord All You Nations G

Elec Gtr Intro

   Final chorus x 2

Great Is Your Faithfulness G

Repeat chorus after

   2nd verse Ska/Reggae

     Feel

We Believe In A Suffering Saviour G

   Full Band Intro

   Drums Count In

   Drop Out final chorus

   Drums and Bass

     Only

If Faith Can Move The Mountains G

   Leave room for Space

   on C/// D///

     Progression

INFO: POSSIBLE THINGS
THAT MAY BE
WRITTEN DURING
A REHEARSAL

All The Room Was Hushed Bb

Build into
   Choruses

How Deep The Father's Love E

AS Written

Thank You, Father E

Build gradually
   Improvise in
   Spaces
     use E major pentatonic

How Great Is Your Love F#m

After Bridge Key change to
BIG $G^\#_m$ chords F# B/D# E

I'm Not Backing Down Em

Break down on
   bridge
"Would you breathe on
   US" Lyric
Bass Build with ♪ quavers

Fig 4 Arrangement Sheet

Chapter 9
Sing a New Song

Sing a new song to the Lord! Sing his praises from the
ends of the earth!
Sing, all you who sail the seas, all you who live in
distant coastlands. (Isaiah 42:10)

Did you know that there are six references to singing a new song in the Bible? There are also one hundred and ten references to the word 'song' and one hundred and fifty-eight uses of the word 'sing'.

Interesting, then, that sung worship is sometimes considered unnecessary and inappropriate by some people. Here's a question. Why did God give us the ability to sing and make music if it wasn't to praise him? Correct me if I'm wrong, but I'm pretty sure the main reason we were put on this earth was to enjoy and worship Him.

Anyway, my point, when I draw your attention to the number of times the Bible refers to singing a new song, is this: it's good to keep singing new songs!

Take the brilliant songs that you didn't write and make them yours – sing a new song, sing your song, sing your church's song, sing your town's song to the Lord.

Let's take a worship song and see it as painting. Let's say that the canvas is the lyrics and melody. Those are your restrictions, the size of your canvas. When it comes to arrangement, style and harmony, you have a blank canvas to paint on! The colours in your paint box are your instruments, your musicians, the brushes. Do you see what I'm getting at?

An exciting prospect for me is the hope that local churches will embrace the musical diversity within their musicians and make their own music and worship culture.

I love the opportunity to visit other churches when I'm on holiday or travelling, because it's interesting to worship in a different place with different roots and a different style.

Embrace it all, it's yours.

Another question. Why is Christian Contemporary Music so narrow in style? Every church will have a team of musicians, with distinct abilities, musical backgrounds and experience. Don't waste it. It's time the local church welcomed its own style, its own voice of worship. Sing a new song!

Chapter 10
Song-writing in the Local Church

*Now write down the words of this song, and teach it to
the people of Israel. Teach them to sing it, so it may
serve as a witness against them.*
(Deuteronomy 31:19)

God asked Moses to write down this song and teach it
because He wasn't very happy with the Israelites. And
that song couldn't have been more authentic to their
situation!

There is something very special about home-
grown worship songs. They are songs that can unify a
church and give the members ownership of the songs
they sing, and let them say, 'This is ours!'

The local church needs to write songs that are
inspired by their localities, written by people who are
living in those places.

Birmingham was the birthplace of Metal music.
The early metal bands say it's because they worked in
factories, and all day would hear the clanking of –

literally – heavy metal. Those sounds influenced the music they were making. Would they have created the music they did if they lived out in the country? You don't hear those sounds out in the fields.

Home worship songs have an authenticity that you can't see in songs from outside. A song written by a person in Australia, America, London or just the next church down the road cannot write as specifically and relevantly for your church as you can.

True, a good worship leader will be able to use songs from outside, and be able to adapt them to speak to the current circumstances of the church. When we play worship, we do this all the time, and that's why sometimes we are guided to rest on a particular lyric or section of a song. Other times a church will take a song to itself for a particular time and it's wonderful that many songs are shared to build up the wider church family.

Song-writing in the local church is something that should happen more, and I think that neighbouring church song writers should get together more to write songs and to share each other's songs around.

If we look at the creation of music in general, we will see that there is a lot of collaboration. Christian music is no exception – song writing teams are springing up more and more. The Compassionart album initiative was an exciting example of this. Many of the most influential worship leaders at the time got together to write worship songs – a testimony to what can be done in our local communities too.

Song-writing shouldn't be exclusive to the worship group either; and perhaps this is where collaboration can come in for us. Elton John wouldn't have had as many hit songs if Bernie Taupin wasn't writing lyrics for him.

Imagine if all the churches, in their various communities, were writing songs together and for each other. For example, what if all the worship leaders in York got together for a session of song-writing or what if a church put on a song-writing day, for church songwriters in that locality?

I'm buzzing about this, I think I'll get in touch with some fellow worship leaders in my community to see about setting a date!

Chapter 11
Rotas—The TAZ Theory

All must give as they are able, according to the
blessings given to them by the Lord your God.
(Deuteronomy 16:17)

Some people may have enough musicians to warrant a rota, others not. A lot of people like the idea of set bands, because you develop an understanding between the musicians – which makes sense. But I love the rota because it means the band is never the same.

It's great to turn up to rehearsal or church on a Sunday and not know what instruments you're going to be using, or who will be wielding them; though obviously, if you're the worship leader you ought to be aware of the musicians in your band and the instruments they play!

In my music degree we studied something called TAZ (Temporary Autonomous Zones). The theory is that for little pockets of time there is an amazing yet fleeting experience. In terms of music history, 'Summer of Love '67' is one, the punk movement is another, Britpop probably the most recent. In my opinion the same can happen with rota worship!

Just think, all these people, from a variety of musical backgrounds, come together once a rota to lead worship for one night only! Imagine if they were free to manifest their unique musical voice. And just think what different styles and genres would come about.

Rota Scenario Potential Worship Band

Drums --------------------- Dave Grohl (Nirvana), Grunge

Bass ------------------ Flea (Red Hot Chili Peppers), Funk

Electric ----------------- Kirk Hammett (Metallica), Metal

Trumpet---------------------------------- Miles Davis, Jazz

Flute --------------------- Ian Anderson (Jethro Tull), Folk

Keyboard ---------------Rick Wakeman (Yes), Prog Rock

Singer---------------------- Morrissey (The Smiths), Indie

Backing singer ----------------- Aretha Franklin, Motown

Crazy! What could you do with all that!? It's intriguing. That's just a generic worship band, and it has eight genres fusing together to facilitate their church's worship. I cannot answer the question. I would be fascinated to hear this band and get an answer!

Chapter 12
Worship Bands are not Tribute Bands

When they came to the other side, Elijah said to Elisha, 'What can I do for you before I am taken away?' And Elisha replied, 'Please let me become your rightful successor. (2 Kings 2:9)

A worship band is not a tribute band! I repeat – not a tribute band!

On a number of occasions I have visited churches that have very large gatherings. Churches with stage lightning, Britney mics and professional musicians, where I've gone not just once but on a succession of Sundays. The band would have the same instrumentation, but different musicians each time. What baffles me is that their song arrangements were exactly the same! Different musicians, different worship leader, yet the music was the same as last Sunday. Not all the songs were the same, granted – and the quality was of the highest standard – but...

'How boring, how tedious, and my soul shall ever sing;
How boring, how tedious is playing when I can't be me!'

I am sure it can't be possible for all the musicians in that church happen to be the same in their style, taste and choice of musical arrangements!

TRIBUTE BAND ALERT!

This leads me to another rant (I'll try to keep it short). Worship leaders who want the band to copy the CD. What's all that about? Unless you've recorded the song with those musicians, then leave it alone! There's no ownership in that!

I don't believe we are meant to be Hillsongs or Worship Central tribute bands. For one thing it's very restrictive on creativity, and on a more practical level it's pretty much impossible to recreate something so specific, because you're not the original musicians playing it.

Now, just to clarify: CDs or YouTube videos of places like this can be an invaluable resource for learning the basics of a song, and a really good basis to build your arrangement from. Nevertheless, from then on, the canvas is yours. You can choose the key you play it in, you could throw in some more jazzy chords, you could add a reggae feel if the structure permits.

Get painting!

However, it must be said that some worship songs have integral instrumental sections that just have to be played. Perhaps you've seen cover bands murder a song by omitting an integral section. My father and I used to enjoy going to local pubs to watch bands. We went to see one particular band and they covered 'Layla' by Derek & The Dominos – and they left out the main riff, the hook! It wasn't the unplugged version, they were a full electric band, but they played it as if it was the unplugged version, but as a 3-piece! It was only in the second chorus that we realised it was 'Layla': in a word, terrible!

In worship music, songs like 'Happy Day' by Tim Hughes without their opening guitar riff would definitely lack something, and these sections are definitely worth keeping in your song arrangements if possible. That said, the guitar doesn't have to play the opening riff – keys can do it, violin etc.

In a nutshell: establish what the hook is in the song and then be creative; making sure that the hook always remains in your arrangement in some shape or form. And if I'm ever asked, I completely condone learning riffs from the CD, because sometimes they really do work.

The main thing is for the motive to be right. What

are we trying to accomplish? Are we trying to create a worshipful environment, or a faithful rendition of a recording?

I agree both can be achieved in certain contexts. I've seen it done many times. But this shouldn't be the ultimate goal. We are not tribute bands, we are cover bands. The difference is that you play other people's songs, but you recreate them to fit the strengths of the musicians within your band.

Jeff Buckley's cover of Leonard Cohen's 'Hallelujah" song would be pointless if it sounded exactly the same as the original. And would Eric Clapton have got a number 1 with his cover of Bob Marley's 'I Shot The Sheriff' if he was faithful to the original recording?

Chapter 13
The Art of Letting Go

The custom of having choir directors to lead choirs in hymns of praise and thanks to God began long ago in the days of David and Asaph. (Nehemiah 12:46)

I recall a time when I had elaborate schemes for the bands I was leading; musical flows and transitions that would take your breath away. From one flawless key change to the next the congregation would be seized by an atmosphere of beauty and musical majesty. But by the time I'd explained the scheme to my band, I'd look at my watch and realise I'd only have three minutes to pray before the service started!

As worship leaders, we need to know when it's time to let go of our vision for what we thought the song could be, and accept what it is becoming.

When I plan worship for a band, I first ascertain the journey we should go on, by praying and asking, 'what does God want to say or do in this time? How, by the end of this worship set, do I prepare the congregation for receiving the word?'

There's no set formula, as long as you're open to the direction of the Holy Spirit. I used to pick a list of songs and make them flow, which is a valid way; sometimes God puts on your heart a song and then you base your worship journey around it.

My worship director suggested that instead of picking the songs first, I should try working out the journey first and then pick songs to fit the journey. This was liberating and made things much easier! I could have my themes and fill in the blanks with songs! I could take into account the band, and pick songs that would fit with their particular qualities as musicians whilst still being true to the journey I was planning.

My arrangements tended to be a little extravagant. So what I do now is to plan the most musically elaborate arrangements that I want – and then I've got that impulse out of my system. Then, I choose one creative thing in those arrangements per song or sometimes per set. In this way, I'm still being innovative and it will actually be possible to put my innovations into practice. For instance, I might put a key change in the final chorus of a song, or have a chorus with just bass and drums, or perhaps an instrumental solo or breakdown in the song.

This way of planning was very helpful, as my rehearsal time was limited and normally there were a lot of songs to get through.

A good thing to do in your rehearsal is to write things down to help you remember. Arrangement sheets are useful. I started making them up because I was tired of getting sheet music that was scribbled with conflicting song ideas, bearing three or more sets of transposed chords that made the sheet music unintelligible.

When I lead a rehearsal now, I tend to specify a feel and then we play through the song. I don't specify particular parts for people to play unless they're really stuck. I talk about dynamics; I say the intro needs to be big, the verses soft, the chorus driving and the bridge needs to drop down or build up, and so on. Of course, if someone is playing a part that doesn't fit, I will ask them to try something else.

We as musicians must also support our leaders by taking an interest in what we can offer to each song, and not waiting for specific direction.

If we take an interest in the music we're playing, then rehearsals will be more fruitful and we will find our time in the band more satisfying.

Chapter 14
Electric Guitar Worship

*Do you see any truly competent workers? They will
serve kings rather than ordinary people.*
(Proverbs 22:29)

I was watching a video on the art of playing electric
guitar in worship. It was a series on effects pedals. At
the point where the worship guitarist stated that you
can only be effective or appropriate as a guitarist in
worship if your pedal board consists of a particular
distortion pedal and another particular delay pedal, I
began wonder what was going on!

So we should all play like U2 and Coldplay should
we? I have a certain appreciation for U2 and Coldplay
– and I own both of those pedals, and use them on my
pedalboard for worship – but what a limitation to *only
use those pedals*. Thousands of Christian guitarists and
the churches they serve are missing out on so much,
simply because of such restrictions and suggestions –
as if playing like U2 or Coldplay is the only way to give

glory to God through sung worship.

All the FX pedals on my board have been bought because another guitarist has excited me with a specific sound, and I wanted to be able to reproduce it. The same can be said with my playing style.

I have a wah-wah pedal because I love how Eric Clapton used it in Cream songs like 'White Room', and also Jimi Hendrix's use of it in on 'Voodoo Child (Slight Return)'.

My chorus/flanger pedal was bought because it has a special function which means you can get a particular tremolo effect which is a favourite of Blur guitarist Graham Coxon, and because on another setting you can get a bluesy reverb tone similar to the sound John Mayer uses on his 'City Love' solo from 'Any Given Thursday'.

I bought my super-shifter pedal because I wanted to recreate some of the squeal sounds that virtuoso guitarists like Joe Satriani and Steve Vai use.

My delay pedal I bought – no, not because it was necessary for worship! I bought it because the guitarist Robert Cray does a solo on his song 'Poor Johnny' where he plays a phrase and then whilst the delay repeats the phrase, he plays another, bouncing off his own ideas in a call-and-response kind of way.

Now, I'm going to throw out a few tips for playing

guitar in a worship context and hopefully after all I've said, that won't make me a hypocrite. I won't be telling you specifically what to play, or what style you should play it in. I'm just going to talk through some basic technique. These can also be useful for worship leaders who lead from the electric guitar.

Sound

It's important and worthwhile to take some time over this. Your amplifier is normally your main point of reference. I won't specify EQs, but you should research the amp settings that your favourite guitarists use. I found Eric Clapton's Cream settings and used them as a starting point, then adapted my settings from there. My settings, if you're interested, are Treb 5, Mid 10, Bass 6. Lots of guitar magazines explain the amp settings used for songs they have transcribed. If you have a favourite guitar sound, you may be able to find it there.

A common trap is that guitarists fail to take into account the fact that their sound is different on their own than when they're playing in a band. Even though excessive amounts of distortion in your bedroom may make you feel like the king of heavy rock, in a band context people will just hear a clarity-free buzz. My favourite way of describing it is that it sounds like wasps in a jar! To avoid this issue, the volume control ought to be a higher setting than the gain. Simply, the higher the gain, and the lower the volume, the more distorted your sound; so it's useful to find the perfect volume-to-gain ratio, so you get that gutsy guitar sound without sacrificing clarity.

Back to FXs again: they are there to enhance your guitar/amp sound, not to replace it. Avoid thinking that a bad amp sound can be remedied by several boxes on the floor. Ultimately they will just enhance your already bad amp sound.

Technique

Electric guitar shouldn't be played the same way as an acoustic. It's not often you need to play all six strings – you can play open chords, but play them by muting or avoiding the open strings rather than using all six.

The electric guitar, when played rhythmically, requires a more controlled approach to basic open strumming. Palm muting needs to mastered, now that your guitar is coming out of an amplifier. You will have more sustain than an acoustic, and this needs to be controlled.

A regular problem is that players' left and right hands do not sync up properly, meaning that the picking hand is ahead of the fretting hand. This makes the notes unclear. The accuracy of the picking hand is especially important when it comes to playing open chords. Hitting rogue open strings which are not part of the chord is not good.

Another common problem is that chords are not fretted properly. Some of the notes in the chord get dampened by the fleshier part of the hand or fingers, with the result that the notes don't ring out. It might be that the fingers are not arched enough. You can get your hand into a better position by raising or lowering your thumb on the neck of the guitar.

To check that your chords are being played cleanly, try plucking each individual string of the chord shape. This will help you identify which (if any) string is being dampened, and you can adjust your hand position accordingly.

Using FXs

Learning the appropriate use of FXs is mainly about trial and error. You don't know what might work in a song until you try. The more extreme FXs need to be used sparingly and with care.

Let's cover the two worship-music favourites.

Firstly, using distortion. Unintentional open strings are a no-no. When playing open chords with distortion, make sure that you are accurate with your picking hand – palm muting is essential in this case. In cases of heavier distortion, removing the 3rd note from the chord and playing the root and 5th – otherwise known as the power chord or 5th chord – can help take out unwanted harmonics that make the chord sound out of tune, particularly when using a heavy metal style rather than an indie rock sound.

Next, delay. Incredibly useful in simple songs which allow for space, or upbeat rock songs that lend themselves to a U2-type vibe. When you're using delay, more complex songs which involve a lot of chord changes are to be avoided, really. Hymns or jazz re-workings which involve chords that might clash with delayed notes can create a harmony mess. Avoid using delay in sections with quick chord changes. And with delay, it's especially important to be accurate with your playing because a mistake will be repeated.

Chain of Importance

Your technique is most important. See your technique as being the materials you'll use to build a house. If you're hitting rogue strings, or your hands don't quite sync up, then the addition of FXs will only show up those issues more clearly and enhance them.

Your amp sound is the foundation on which

everything is built. It is your main sound and if that isn't right, then again, FXs will only make it worse.

Finally, add your FXs. I guess they're your furnishings and so on. If everything else in the chain is as it should be, then these FXs, calibrated and used in the right places, will make you sound brilliant!

A final thought on FXs – it's worth taking the time to be sure that both your playing and your amp are up to it before buying FX pedals.

Chapter 15
Improvisation—Nothing to Fear

O Lord, I'm just not a good speaker. I never have been, and I'm not now, even after you have spoken to me. I'm clumsy with words. (Exodus 4:10)

In my experience of being on worship teams, doing a music degree and teaching guitar, I have found that many of my fellow musicians have a real fear of improvisation.

It's not that these musicians are incapable. They're fully equipped to be very skilled improvisers. I know of Grade Eight musicians who can play any notated music you put in front of them; yet put in front of them a sheet of four chords and ask them to improvise and they would look at you confused and a little embarrassed.

Who makes mouths?' the Lord asked him. 'Who makes people so they can speak or not speak, hear or not hear, see or not see? Is it not I, the

Lord? Now go, and do as I have told you. I will help you speak well, and I will tell you what to say. (Exodus 4:11-12)

I'm using Moses as an example because he had the tools to do God's work. He had a mouth. I believe it's the same with musicians and improvising.

What tools do we need to improvise? All we need is to know some scales. Many musicians know their scales backwards – but the scales have just been used as finger exercises rather than tools for making music!

Two of my current students were learning scales and they were fearful of improvisation. They each said, 'I'm rubbish at improvising.' After learning a few scales and putting some work into it, they are now fluent improvisers, and certainly able to improvise over a basic worship song.

The fear is a fear of having to make something up on the spot. That fear is unjustified. There can be a belief that there's some kind of magic which comes upon us in that moment and we create something that no person has played before. It's not true. Pretty much everything we play in that or any other moment we will have played before!

Improvisation comes from trial and error in your own personal practice time. When you improvise in public, you'll be using the phrases that you've worked out in practice. As you practice improvising you will build up a 'phrase library', and this library will consist of phrases which work over different chords and keys. All we're doing when we improvise is sifting through the phrases in our library and choosing which ones to use at that point.

Your library will mainly come from listening to and learning from your favourite musicians. So when you're taking the time to learn a piece of music, and there's a phrase that jumps out at you, why not add it to your phrase library? Take the music you have taken the trouble to learn, cut it up into phrases and make your own new phrases from the pieces

All my playing is by numbers. Some people can hear in their head what they want to play, and then make that come out of their instrument. I do that to an extent, but it's more that I've played a certain phrase over this chord or this key before and it worked – so logic suggests it will work again.

There is of course some theory involved, and the more you progress and practice sequences with more creative chords, the more you will develop your capacity for understanding and using particular scales. But for our purposes, I am going to share Eric Clapton's – and every guitarist's – favourite, the pentatonic scale (see Pentatonic Sheet). This scale consists of 5 notes. Most scales consist of 7 notes (Ionian (Major), Aeolian (Minor), Dorian, Mixolydian, Lydian, Phrygian, Locrian). A pentatonic scale is a subset of those 7 notes – the same scale but with 2 notes missed out. The great thing is that the pentatonic is missing the 2 notes which tend to be the bad notes if they're played in the wrong place. Which means that provided you are in the right key, all the notes in that scale will work over any chord in that key! The key can normally be worked out from the first chord in the music.

The instrument you play will obviously change the types of techniques and expressions you can reproduce, and you can learn by listening to your favourite improvisers on your instrument, as well as doing a bit of research.

I recommend practicing at home by playing along to backing tracks on YouTube. Search for backing tracks in whichever key you wish to try, use the diagram in this chapter to make sure you know the notes of the scale, and give it a go!

Fig 5. Pentatonic Scale Sheet

Major Pentatonic Scale

T   T   T½   T   T   T½

Minor Pentatonic Scale

T½   T   T   T½   T

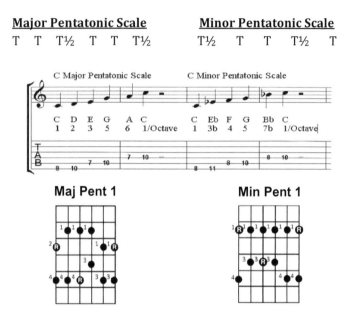

MAJOR KEY (Circle of 5ths)	MAJOR PENTATONIC	MINOR KEY (Circle of 5ths)	MINOR PENTATONIC
C (0)	C D E F G A (C)	Am (0)	A C D E F G (A)
G (1#)	G A B D E (G)	Em (1#)	E G A B D (E)
D (2#)	D E F# A B (D)	Bm (2#)	B D E F# A (B)
A (3#)	A B C# E F# (A)	F#m (3#)	F# A B C# E (F#)
E (4#)	E F# G# B C# (E)	C#m (4#)	C# E F# G# B (C#)

B (5#)	B C# D# F# G# (B)	G#m (5#)	G# B C# D# F# (G#)
F# (6#) or Gb	F# G# A# C# D# (F#)	D#m (6#) or Ebm	D# F# G# A# C# (D#)
MAJOR KEY (Circle of 4ths)		**MINOR KEY (Circle of 4ths)**	
C (0)	See C above	Am (0)	See Am above
F (1b)	F G A C D (F)	Dm (1b)	D F G A C (D)
Bb (2b)	Bb C D F G (Bb)	Gm (2b)	G Bb C D F (G)
Eb (3b)	Eb F G Bb C (Eb)	Cm (3b)	C Eb F G Bb (C)
Ab (4b)	Ab Bb C Eb F (Ab)	Fm (4b)	F Ab Bb C Eb (F)
Db (5b)	Db Eb F Ab Bb (Db)	Bbm (5b)	Bb Db Eb F Ab (Bb)
Gb (6b) or F#	Gb Ab Bb Db Eb (Gb)	Ebm (6b) or D#m	Eb Gb Ab Bb Db (Eb)

Chapter 16
No Solos in Worship?

And whenever the tormenting spirit from God troubled Saul, David would play the harp. Then Saul would feel better, and the tormenting spirit would go away.
(1 Samuel 16:23)

I attended a gathering of worship leaders, and our host was talking about how their church led worship, did team-building and so on. At one point he said something that made me a little irritated. 'We've been taking a serious look at how we do worship on a Sunday, and we've decided that there should be no guitar solos. We feel that the congregation are less engaged when they're taking place.'

My irritation is not (entirely) because I'm an electric guitarist. I don't believe I should have a solo in every song of every service. But I feel that there shouldn't be such a rigid rule, one which could easily result in stifled creativity.

Ironically, not five minutes earlier, the host had said that their church musicians were encouraged to get lessons, and he made a particular point of mentioning electric guitarists. But if they're not allowed to rejoice in their gifts, what's the point?

No doubt there are some guitar fans in the congregation who appreciate guitar solos, and may even feel they engage and connect more with God during them. I myself have been made more fully aware of God's holiness and majesty during a trumpet solo at a worship event.

Have you ever been in a place that was so beautiful that all you can think is that God is good? Or have you walked into a cathedral with awe and been moved to the almighty? Do we not engage with the arts in much the same way?

Of course, there are times when solos are inappropriate, and the attitude surrounding any creativity in worship has to be that of a humble servant. This means, I'm afraid, that lifting the guitar over your head is the wrong attitude. I know, I know, it's a shame.

You may have heard the term 'ministry song', meaning a song which is played to give people a space to reflect on the message and engage without singing. I would suggest that if ministry songs are useful, then guitar solos or any instrumental solos can also be useful.

Chapter 17
Church Music Isn't Enough

Wherever your treasure is, there your heart and thoughts will also be. (Luke 12:34)

Sometimes, I have felt the frustration whilst worshipping that I am unable to put into practice the things I have learned at my guitar lessons. I am also fortunate that sometimes I can!

But the things I learn in guitar lessons rarely, if ever, come from church music. If you want to develop as a musician, church music isn't enough.

If you are a keen musician and are looking for a challenge, I would advise you not to look for it in a worship group. The end result will be dissatisfaction and frustration. Our role as worship musicians is to serve the church, not to fulfil our own musical aspirations.

Church music can, however, be rewarding, and it is always important. But the simplicity of it leaves you an opportunity to get involved in making music outside of your church, and in the process to nourish yourself as a musician. This is also fruitful for the church music group you're in. As well as not being a disappointed troublemaker, you will be bringing more experience and knowledge to your worship group.

There's another opportunity when our worship groups aren't the only place we play music. We can create music groups within our churches, like the small groups where we meet together to grow and have fellowship in addition to going to church on a Sunday. Why not have fellowship in playing music with people too – not for performance in church but just for the joy of playing?

At my church there are a number of times through the year when music is required for outreach events. There are usually musicians thrown together in a group to make music for these occasions. In our church, the two main opportunities come at Christmas and Easter. We have church cafes, which put on mini-services of about twenty minutes throughout the day, and normally we have a gospel choir supported by a band.

The gospel choir was formed by a member of the music group and some keen vocalists. It has now turned into a singers group, covering more genres than just gospel. I had the joy of being able to play electric guitar in the band that supported the gospel choir at these cafes. I mentioned to the choir leader afterwards that it'd be good to have a set gospel band that would practice at choir rehearsals. Before I knew what was happening an email was sent round saying that I was now in charge of organising the gospel band! I don't remember saying I would organise it, but I just needed a little push.

I put together a gospel band and we supported the choir. We also tried to get together once a month to play some big-band pieces, and any other music that the band members liked to play. We had a really good time playing together, and I think we found it beneficial. It was also a pleasure for me to record, with this band, a worship song I had written.

Along with this, we organised a jam every month or so on a Friday night, where musicians from the team could come and play music with each other. It was great fun, and it was inspiring to hear and see the strengths of the musicians in the group as they played music they really enjoyed.

Music has so many outreach possibilities, whether it's to be entertained by, or to get involved in. Put on some concerts at your church and bless your community! Why don't you become the person who gets the ball rolling at your church?

Chapter 18
Song Keys for Congregations

But among you, those who are the greatest
should take the lowest rank and the leader
should be like a servant. (Luke 22:26)

As a worship group our primary responsibility is to lift Jesus high and serve the people in our church. This would suggest that the congregation's needs take priority over our own.

At my church we take pains to work out singable keys for each song. The point of this is that men and women have different vocal ranges and it is beneficial to find the key which works for both.

Many new worship songs have octave jumps, so selecting keys for these songs becomes difficult. The verse tune starts in a singable register, not too low for men and not too high for women, but then the chorus has an octave jump and suddenly women will be screeching because they have to sing the octave above the male octave, and the original song keys can make it a strain for men to get up there too. In the same way, if you drop the song to a lower key so you can sing the chorus comfortably, then often the verse will become too low to sing.

Hymns do not tend to have this problem, as their melodies tend to stay in a specific octave and tend not to have too many jumps to the top note. They're usually gradual, and work their way up the scale, which makes singing easier – and most hymns are in singable keys to begin with.

At my church, the worship director's rule was to keep the tune between an A at the bottom and an E flat at the top, pushing down to a G and up to an E when necessary.

The absolute safe range is a B at the bottom and a C# at the top; however, that is overly cautious and will probably be too great a restriction on many of the songs you could sing, especially when it comes to songs with octave jumps.

We should take into account the fact that not everyone in our congregations will be musical, or will have a large vocal range. In order to facilitate their sung worship, it is important to pick keys that are sympathetic to them. If a song is too high, members of your congregation could feel self-conscious. Similarly, if a song is too low, members of the congregation will struggle to project their voices.

Another thing to consider when leading is the time of day and the number of people in the congregation.

When I lead worship at an early-morning prayer meeting, I tend to drop the key of each song I choose by a tone – so A would become G, for example. However, if the song involves octave jumps, be wary of dropping the key down, particularly if you have already put those songs in congregationally friendly keys.

I played 'You Alone Can Rescue' by Matt Redman at a morning prayer-meeting, in the key of G. The original is in the key of B, and my church tends to lead it in Bb or A, so I had to do a key change mid-song to knock it up to A because I was singing in my boots; it was too low. I have also had the experience of leading a song and realising that it's too high for people at that time in the morning, and knocking it down a key.

You can have quite a lot of fun with impromptu key changes mid-worship (though it's usually only a good idea to do it when you're leading by yourself!). Once, leading an early-morning prayer meeting, I used a song as a vocal warm-up. It was 'Thank You, Father' by Gareth Robinson. It has three sections. The first thanks the Father. The next thanks the Son and finally, the Spirit. The song is originally in the key of E, so I did the first section in C, then the next in D and the final section in E: a key change between each section. We were all warming our voices up together, it was fun!

In evening services, I tend to stick to the original keys, as most people's voices are at their peak.

It's also important to consider the number of people in the congregation. In a small, intimate setting, I take a gentle approach. In a smaller gathering people can be more self-conscious, and so I will pick keys which don't need too much volume to hit the higher notes.

In a large venue with thousands of people, the band are so loud that you can't hear what you and the person next to you are singing. In that context it doesn't matter what keys you use, because there's less scope for people to feel self-conscious about being heard.

At a conference or large church, those leading worship will pick keys that make their vocals sound the best they possibly can, rather than picking keys for congregations. I think in that context that's absolutely fine, and very wise. Saying this, at my parents' church – which isn't huge – they sing most songs in the original key and no one seems bothered by it, they just go for it. That's a good attitude to have!

It can be intimidating to think about transposing music if you've never done it before. But there are a number of websites that can transpose music for you[2] and most worship song books contain a CD which allows you to transpose the songs in the book using your computer. Alternatively, take a look at the 'How to Transpose' section at the end of this chapter.

In my context, I'm all for picking keys to help the congregation. If I was leading at a large worship event – which is more like a concert – then I would pick keys that would help me to sound my best.

I believe both ways are valid and can equally serve your congregation, depending on the context you are in. My parents' church worships God vibrantly and even though when I'm there I'm often thinking, 'This is a high key for this time in the morning,' it doesn't stop them!

Fig. 6 How To Transpose Sheet

KEY (NUMBER OF # Sharps OR b Flats)	CHORD I (ROOT)	CHORD II (MINOR)	CHORD III (MINOR)	CHORD IV (MAJOR)	CHORD V (MAJOR)	CHORD VI (RELATIVE MINOR)	CHORD VII (DIMINISHED)
C (no # sharps or b flats)	C	Dm	Em	F	G	Am	Bm7b5
Db (5bs or 5 Flats)	Db	Ebm	Fm	Gb	Ab	Bbm	Cm7b5
D (2# or 2 Sharps)	D	Em	F#m	G	A	Bm	C#m7b5
Eb (3bs or 3 Flats)	Eb	Fm	Gm	Ab	Bb	Cm	Dm7b5
E (4# or 4 Sharps)	E	F#m	G#m	A	B	C#m	D#m7b5

F (1b or 1 Flat)	F	Gm	Am	Bb	C	Dm	Em7b5
F# (6# or 6 Sharps)	F#	G#m	A#m	B	C#	D#m	E#m7b5
G (1# or 1 Sharp)	G	Am	Bm	C	D	Em	F#m7b5
Ab (4bs or 4 Flats)	Ab	Bbm	Cm	Db	Eb	Fm	Gm7b5
A (3# or 3 Sharps)	A	Bm	C#m	D	E	F#m	G#m7b5
Bb (2bs or 2 Flats)	Bb	Cm	Dm	Eb	F	Gm	Am7b5
B (5# or 5 Sharps)	B	C#m	D#m	E	F#	G#m	A#m7b5

Firstly, we must identify the key. In order to do this compare the chords in the song with the chart above.

Let's say that this song is in the key of A and we want to change it to G.

The chord sequence for the Verse is A F#m D E. In the chart, the chord A is Chord I (Root). F#m is Chord VI (Relative Minor). D is Chord IV (Major and finally E is Chord V (Major).

To transpose to G as you can see in the chart Chord I (Root) will now be G. Chord VI (Relative Minor) will now be Em. Chord IV (Major) is C and Chord V (Major) is D.

You can use this chart to help you transpose and eventually you'll understand the patterns and be able to transpose without the help of this sheet.

Chapter 19
The Techy-Muso War

Share each other's troubles and problems,
and in this way obey the law of Christ.
(Galatians 6:2)

I'm pretty sure everyone who works with church music has experienced this conflict. Sound engineers and musicians, in church, at each other's throats. The musicians can't hear enough through the monitors on stage, the sound engineers can't get a good mix because the musicians are too loud, and so on.

I do both jobs at my church, and I would recommend that worship musicians should at least attend a sound-tech training session or go to a tech seminar at a conference, even if they have no intention of joining the technical team. Just by taking one evening out of your schedule you could avoid becoming a casualty on this battlefield.

The main cause of this war is that, we fear what we do not understand. Musicians do not understand which wire plugs into where, and sound engineers don't understand about getting the vibe, man.

A healthy respect for one another is needed. We as musicians may sometimes feel that what we do is more important than what the sound engineers do. We feel that they are our servants and should bow to our wishes. The sound engineers feel like they are servants to ungrateful masters and that they get blamed for everything.

The thing that really frustrates both factions is that we are dependent on one another. The musicians won't sound good at the front without our sound engineers, and without musicians there would be no sound to engineer at all.

> *If you think you are too important to help someone in need, you are only fooling yourself. You are really nobody.* (Galatians 6:3)

Strong words from Paul in his letter to the Galatians; and perhaps you're thinking 'Steady on, Phil, we don't think that!'

I'm sure that's true to an extent. I know I used to struggle with sound engineers, and, feeling like I was the star, I would become very annoyed at the end of a gig or service when I would ask a friend, 'Did it sound alright?'

I'm afraid musicians seek affirmation and there's nothing worse than getting the response 'Yeah, it sounded good, couldn't really hear **you**, though.' Arrrghh! I may as well have not bothered!

On the flip-side of this argument, try thanking the sound engineer after the service. It will make their week! If a sound engineer does a good job, they tend not to receive any recognition for it. If something goes wrong, every head will turn in their direction.

Occasionally when I've been sound engineering, I have had people thank me for my mix, and it feels great. Interestingly, a lot of that has to do with the musicians on stage. As my music college tutor, whose specialty was sound-engineering, once said to me: 'You can't polish a turd.' Crude, but accurate nonetheless. If the band plays badly, it doesn't matter how much you tweak the EQ, the volume or FXs; they are going to sound rubbish, and you are most likely going to make it worse.

Another classic is for a musician to say, 'Oh, the sound was all wrong today, it sounded rubbish!' The only response can be, 'How do you know? You weren't out there in pews.'

It's a common misconception that what you hear in the monitor mix reflects the sound going out to the congregation. It doesn't. Most monitor mixes will be dry (without FXs) - you will be getting back your pure sound, and probably not even hearing the band in its entirety.

I've seen both sides of the coin, and both jobs present their challenges; and things are much better when both parties understand each other's purpose. Since I have an understanding of what it's like to do both, when I'm on stage I know that turning my amp up excessively will not benefit those mixing the front of house; and as a sound engineer I recognise that those on stage require a certain ambience.

This ambience is a little hard to explain. Basically, you need a monitor mix that isn't deafening, yet has enough volume to support the musicians on stage, so no one in the band feels overly exposed, and everyone can play without reservation.

Musicians and sound engineers are both there to serve their church with their skills, so let's work on this relationship – whose importance is not to be understated. It could make the difference between your congregation's engagement in worship and their distraction from it.

Chapter 20
Why do we do it?

Let the godly sing with joy to the Lord, for it is fitting to praise him. Praise the Lord with melodies on the lyre; make music for him on the ten-stringed harp. Sing new songs of praise to him; play skillfully on the harp and sing with joy. (Psalm 33:1-3)

I would argue that Psalm 33 expresses pretty much every reason why we stand up to lead worship on a Sunday.

It starts with the fact that as worship musicians, we have a responsibility to praise the Lord. Not only to praise Him, but to do it skilfully, and to sing new songs. You could replace the lyre or the ten-stringed harp with your own instrument in Psalm 33; 'new songs' could mean your own self-penned worship songs, or a new interpretation of the songs you play each week in church.

> *Let everyone in the world fear the Lord, and let everyone stand in awe of him.* (Psalm 33:8-9)

There is a challenge here for us to take our service to God and to our congregation seriously. It is important that we use and develop the talents that we have been given, and keep revealing the mysteries of the Father, the Son and the Holy Spirit with fresh expressions of worship, not only for the congregation we serve, but also for the world.

> *For the word of the Lord holds true, and everything he does is worthy of our trust.*
> *He loves whatever is just and good and his unfailing love fills the earth.*
> *The Lord merely spoke, and the heavens were created. He breathed the word, and all the stars were born. He gave the sea its boundaries and locked the oceans in vast reservoirs.*
> (Psalm 33:4-7)

We worship Him because, as verses 6 and 7 tell us, He is the creator, God the Almighty, deserving worship simply for being who He is! But as well as this, he is, as we read in verses 4 and 5, utterly worthy of our trust; he is just and true and His love for us is unfailing!

> *We depend on the Lord alone to save us. Only he can help us, protecting us like a shield. In Him our hearts rejoice, for we are trusting in his holy name.*
>
> *Let your unfailing love surround us, Lord, for our hope is in you alone.* (Psalm 33:20-22)

And finally, the big winner: salvation! Through engagement with God we can see Him more fully and see our circumstances and hearts changed.

As musicians and worshippers, then, we are using our gifts for a good purpose! I love it, I would hate to give it up. I'm a musician, and using my gifts in music in church is a massive part of how I worship God.

A final thought, though. A couple of years ago I broke my wrist whilst playing football, and I had to wear a plaster cast. For six weeks I couldn't play the guitar. It was really difficult in some ways because I couldn't play; but in other ways it was a good break, because it forced me to take some time and get some perspective on why I was playing church music in the first place. Not primarily because of my gifts, but because of God's glory.

We do it all for Him!

REFERENCES

[1] www.youtube.com/watch?v=hK-BU7AZeZs or www.leadworship.com (for DVD resources)

[2] www.praisecharts.com
www.thetabulator.com
www.autotransposer.com
www.quicktranspositions.com

If you would like to contact Philip, please email him at pmauthor@outlook.com or visit his web page at www.gileadbookspublishing/philip-mckenning